Table of Contents

Preface 1

1. Introduction to Artificial Intelligence 5

1.1 Definition of Artificial Intelligence 5

1.2 History of AI 5

    Origins (1940s-1950s) 6

    Birth of AI (1950s-1970s) 6

    AI Winters (1970s-1990s) 6

    AI Renaissance (1990s-present) 7

1.3 Types of AI 7

    Narrow AI 7

    General AI 7

    Superintelligence 8

1.4 AI Domains and Subdomains 8

    Machine Learning (ML) 8

    Natural Language Processing (NLP) 8

    Computer Vision 8

    Robotics and Autonomous Systems 9

    Planning and Optimization 9

1.5 AI Tools and Technologies 9

1.6 Impact of AI on Society 10

    Economic Transformation: 10

    Employment: 10

    Healthcare: 10

    Education: 10

    Privacy and Security: 11

    Ethical Considerations: 11

    Social Impact: 11

1.7 Conclusion 12

2. **Chapter 2: Theoretical Foundations of AI 13**
   2.1 Introduction 13
   2.2 Algorithms and Data Structures 13
      Basic Algorithms 13
      Data Structures 14
   2.3 Machine Learning 14
      Supervised Learning 15
      Unsupervised Learning 15
      Reinforcement Learning 15
   2.4 Neural Networks and Deep Learning 16
      Artificial Neural Networks (ANN) 16
      Convolutional Neural Networks (CNN) 17
      Recurrent Neural Networks (RNN) 17
   2.5 Theories of Learning 17
      Statistical Learning Theory 17
      Bayesian Learning 18
   2.6 Conclusion 18

3. **Machine Learning Techniques 19**
   3.1 Introduction 19
   3.2 Supervised Learning 19
      Linear Regression 19
      Logistic Regression 20
      Decision Trees 20
      Random Forests 20
      Support Vector Machines (SVM) 20
   3.3 Unsupervised Learning 21
      Clustering 21
      Dimensionality Reduction 21

3.4 Reinforcement Learning 21
Q-learning 22
Deep Q Networks (DQN) 22
3.5 Deep Learning 22
Convolutional Neural Networks (CNN) 22
Recurrent Neural Networks (RNN) 23
Generative Adversarial Networks (GAN) 23
3.6 Transfer Learning 23
Pre-trained Models 23
3.7 Model Evaluation and Selection 24
Evaluation Metrics 24
Cross-Validation 24
3.8 Conclusion 25

4. Applications of AI 26
4.1 Introduction 26
4.2 Healthcare 26
Medical Imaging 26
Personalized Medicine 27
Drug Discovery 27
4.3 Finance 27
Algorithmic Trading 27
Fraud Detection 28
Customer Service 28
4.4 Transportation 28
Autonomous Vehicles 28
Traffic Management 29
Logistics and Supply Chain 29
4.5 Retail 29
Personalized Recommendations 29
Inventory Management 30

  Customer Service 30
4.6 Manufacturing 30
  Quality Control 30
  Predictive Maintenance 31
  Supply Chain Optimization 31
4.7 Education 31
  Personalized Learning 31
  Administrative Tasks 32
  Student Performance Analysis 32
4.8 Entertainment 32
  Content Creation 32
  Personalized Recommendations 33
  Enhanced User Experiences 33
4.9 Conclusion 33
5. AI in the Real World 34
5.1 Introduction 34
5.2 Data Management 34
  Data Collection 34
  Data Preprocessing 34
  Data Storage 35
5.3 Model Development 35
  Algorithm Selection 35
  Hyperparameter Tuning 36
  Model Training 36
5.4 Deployment 36
  Model Serving 36
  Scalability 36
  Security 37
5.5 Monitoring and Maintenance 37
  Performance Monitoring 37

  Model Retraining 37
  Error Analysis 38
 5.6 Ethical and Legal Considerations 38
  Bias and Fairness 38
  Transparency and Explainability 38
  Privacy and Security 39
 5.7 Conclusion 39

6. Ethics and Challenges of AI 40
 6.1 Introduction 40
 6.2 Bias and Fairness 40
  Sources of Bias 40
  Mitigating Bias 41
 6.3 Privacy and Security 41
  Data Privacy 41
  Security Risks 41
 6.4 Transparency and Explainability 42
  Importance 42
  Techniques 42
 6.5 Impact on Employment 42
  Job Displacement 42
  Job Creation 43
 6.6 Societal Impact 43
  Positive Impacts 43
  Negative Impacts 43
 6.7 Ethical Frameworks and Guidelines 44
  Principles 44
  Organizations and Initiatives 44
  6.8 Conclusion 45

7. The Future of AI 46
 7.1 Introduction 46

7.2 Emerging Trends 46
AI and Internet of Things (IoT) 46
Edge AI 46
AI in Healthcare 47
Natural Language Processing (NLP) 47
7.3 Potential Breakthroughs 47
General AI 48
Quantum Computing and AI 48
Brain-Computer Interfaces (BCI) 48
7.4 Long-Term Impact 48
Economic Transformation 49
Societal Changes 49
Global Collaboration 49

Glossary 51
References 53

Preface

Artificial Intelligence (AI) is rapidly transforming our world, ushering in a new era of technological advancement that promises to revolutionize every aspect of our lives. From healthcare to finance, from education to entertainment, AI is reshaping industries, driving innovation, and offering unprecedented opportunities for improving human well-being. As we stand on the cusp of this technological revolution, it is crucial to understand the fundamentals of AI, its applications, and the ethical and societal implications it brings.

This book, "The Foundations and Future of Artificial Intelligence," aims to provide a comprehensive guide to the field of AI. It is designed for a diverse audience, including students, researchers, professionals, and anyone interested in understanding the profound impact of AI on our world. Our goal is to offer a clear and accessible introduction to the key concepts, methodologies, and applications of AI, while also addressing the challenges and ethical considerations that accompany its development and deployment.

The book is structured to take the reader on a journey through the multifaceted landscape of AI. We begin with the historical context and foundational theories that have shaped AI, providing a solid grounding in its origins and core principles. From there, we delve into the various techniques and algorithms that underpin modern AI, offering insights into how these technologies work and how they are applied in real-world scenarios.

One of the central themes of this book is the practical application of AI across different industries. We explore how AI is being used to solve complex problems, enhance efficiency, and create new opportunities in fields such as healthcare, finance, transportation, and beyond. By examining specific case studies and examples, we aim to illustrate the tangible benefits and potential of AI, while also highlighting the challenges and limitations that must be addressed.

Another critical aspect of this book is the exploration of the ethical and societal implications of AI. As AI systems become more integrated into our daily lives, it is essential to consider issues of fairness, transparency, privacy, and accountability. We discuss the potential risks and unintended consequences of AI, and propose frameworks and guidelines for ensuring its responsible and equitable development.

Looking ahead, we also examine the future trajectory of AI, identifying emerging trends and potential breakthroughs that could shape the next wave of innovation. From advancements in natural language processing and quantum computing to the integration of AI with the Internet of Things, we offer a forward-looking perspective on the possibilities and challenges that lie ahead.

In writing this book, we have drawn upon a wealth of knowledge and expertise from leading researchers, practitioners, and thought leaders in the field of AI. Our aim is to present this information in a clear and engaging manner, making it accessible to readers with varying levels of familiarity with AI.

We hope that this book will serve as a valuable resource for anyone seeking to understand the transformative impact of AI, and inspire further exploration and innovation in this exciting and rapidly evolving field.

Thank you for embarking on this journey with us. We are excited to explore the world of artificial intelligence together, and to envision a future where AI contributes to a better, more equitable, and prosperous world.

1. Introduction to Artificial Intelligence

1.1 Definition of Artificial Intelligence

Artificial Intelligence (AI) is a branch of computer science focused on creating systems capable of performing tasks that would normally require human intelligence. This includes abilities such as learning, reasoning, perception, understanding natural language, and decision-making.

AI can be defined in various ways depending on the context and objectives of its use. A general definition is: "Artificial Intelligence is the science and engineering of making intelligent machines, especially intelligent computer programs." This definition highlights the main goal of AI: endowing machines with capabilities similar to those of humans.

1.2 History of AI

The history of AI is marked by several key milestones and innovations:

Origins (1940s-1950s)

- **1943:** Warren McCulloch and Walter Pitts publish a paper on neural networks, laying the theoretical foundations of AI.

- **1950:** Alan Turing proposes the "Turing Test" in his paper "Computing Machinery and Intelligence," suggesting that if a machine can imitate human responses indistinguishably, it could be considered intelligent.

Birth of AI (1950s-1970s)

- **1956:** The Dartmouth Conference is considered the founding event of AI. John McCarthy, Marvin Minsky, Nathaniel Rochester, and Claude Shannon attend and propose the term "Artificial Intelligence."

- **1960s:** Development of the first AI programs, such as Allen Newell and Herbert A. Simon's Logic Theorist and Joseph Weizenbaum's ELIZA, a natural language processing program.

AI Winters (1970s-1990s)

- **1970s-1980s:** High expectations and limited results lead to reduced funding and interest in AI, a period known as the "AI Winter."

- **1980s:** Expert systems, which use specialized knowledge bases to make decisions, revive interest in AI.

AI Renaissance (1990s-present)

- 1990s: Advances in computing and data processing enable significant progress. IBM's Deep Blue defeats world chess champion Garry Kasparov in 1997.

- 2000s-present: Explosion of data and computing power, along with advances in deep learning, propel AI to new heights. Google DeepMind creates AlphaGo, which defeats the world champion of Go in 2016.

1.3 Types of AI

AI can be classified into three main categories: narrow AI, general AI, and superintelligence.

Narrow AI

Narrow AI, also known as weak AI, is specialized in a specific task. It is designed to perform a single function or a limited set of functions. Examples: voice assistants like Siri and Alexa, Netflix or Amazon recommendation systems, and facial recognition software.

General AI

General AI, or Artificial General Intelligence (AGI), is a form of AI capable of understanding, learning, and applying knowledge autonomously, similar to human intelligence. AGI is not yet a reality but represents the ultimate goal of many AI researchers.

Superintelligence

Superintelligence refers to an intelligence that surpasses the best human brains in almost every field, including scientific creativity, general wisdom, and social skills. It remains theoretical for now and raises many ethical and existential debates.

1.4 AI Domains and Subdomains

AI encompasses several subdomains, each with specific applications and techniques:

Machine Learning (ML)

- Techniques of supervised, unsupervised, and reinforcement learning
- Applications: prediction, classification, regression, clustering

Natural Language Processing (NLP)

- Understanding and generating text
- Applications: chatbots, sentiment analysis, machine translation

Computer Vision

- Image and video recognition
- Applications: medical diagnosis, surveillance, autonomous driving

Robotics and Autonomous Systems

- Design of robots capable of perceiving and interacting with their environment
- Applications: industrial robots, drones, autonomous vehicles

Planning and Optimization

- Solving complex problems through planning and optimization
- Applications: logistics, supply chain management, urban planning

1.5 AI Tools and Technologies

AI relies on a variety of tools and technologies, including:
- Programming Languages: Python, R, Java
- Libraries and Frameworks: TensorFlow, PyTorch, Scikit-learn
- Development Environments: Jupyter Notebooks, Google Colab
- Computing Infrastructures: GPU, cloud computing

1.6 Impact of AI on Society

The impact of AI on society is profound and multifaceted, influencing various aspects of our daily lives, economy, and culture. Here are some key impacts:

Economic Transformation: AI is reshaping industries by automating tasks, optimizing processes, and creating new job roles in fields like data science and AI development. It enhances productivity and efficiency across sectors, contributing to economic growth.

Employment: While AI creates new job opportunities in technical and AI-related fields, it also raises concerns about job displacement due to automation. Roles requiring routine tasks are particularly vulnerable, necessitating reskilling and adaptation in the workforce.

Healthcare: AI enables advancements in medical diagnostics, personalized treatment plans, and drug discovery. It improves patient outcomes, enhances medical research capabilities, and contributes to more efficient healthcare delivery.

Education: AI is transforming education through personalized learning experiences, adaptive tutoring systems, and data-driven insights into student performance. It supports lifelong learning and expands access to quality education globally.

Privacy and Security: The widespread use of AI raises concerns about data privacy, cybersecurity, and the ethical use of personal information. Safeguarding data and developing robust AI systems resistant to adversarial attacks are critical challenges.

Ethical Considerations: AI systems can perpetuate biases present in training data, leading to unfair outcomes. Ensuring fairness, transparency, and accountability in AI decision-making is essential to mitigate these ethical issues.

Social Impact: AI influences social interactions, cultural norms, and ethical values. It prompts discussions on autonomy, job displacement, and the equitable distribution of AI benefits. Addressing these societal impacts requires collaborative efforts across stakeholders.

Understanding these impacts helps navigate the opportunities and challenges posed by AI, ensuring its development benefits society while addressing ethical, privacy, and economic considerations.

1.7 Conclusion

Artificial intelligence is a rapidly evolving field transforming many aspects of our daily and professional lives. Understanding its foundations, applications, and implications is essential to navigate a world increasingly influenced by this technology. The following chapters will delve deeper into the various facets of AI, from machine learning techniques to the ethical challenges it poses.

2. Chapter 2: Theoretical Foundations of AI

2.1 Introduction

To fully understand artificial intelligence, it is crucial to grasp the theoretical foundations that underpin it. This chapter explores the essential concepts and techniques that form the basis of AI, including algorithms, data structures, and various learning methods.

2.2 Algorithms and Data Structures

Algorithms and data structures are the building blocks of AI. An algorithm is a set of rules or instructions designed to solve a problem or perform a task. Data structures, on the other hand, organize and store data in ways that facilitate its use.

Basic Algorithms

- Linear Search: Traverses a list element by element to find a target value.
- Binary Search: Divides a sorted list in half to locate a target value, reducing the number of elements to compare.

- Sorting: Algorithms such as quicksort, mergesort, and heapsort organize data in a specific order.

Data Structures

- Arrays: Collection of elements of the same type, accessible by an index.
- Linked Lists: Sequence of elements where each element points to the next.
- Stacks and Queues: Linear data structures for managing collections of elements, following LIFO (Last In, First Out) for stacks and FIFO (First In, First Out) for queues.
- Trees: Hierarchical structure where each node has one or more children, such as binary trees and binary search trees (BST).
- Graphs: Set of nodes connected by edges, used to represent complex relationships and networks.

2.3 Machine Learning

Machine learning is a subfield of AI that enables machines to learn from data and improve with experience without being explicitly programmed. It can be divided into three main categories: supervised learning, unsupervised learning, and reinforcement learning.

Supervised Learning

- Definition: Supervised learning involves training a model on a labeled dataset, where each training example is associated with a correct answer.
- Techniques:
  - Linear Regression: Models the relationship between a dependent variable and one or more independent variables.
  - Decision Trees: Uses a tree-like structure to make decisions based on features.
  - Random Forests: Combines multiple decision trees to improve accuracy and reduce overfitting.
  - Support Vector Machines (SVM): Classifies data by maximizing the margin between different categories.

Unsupervised Learning

- Definition: Unsupervised learning trains models on data without labels, allowing the algorithm to discover hidden structures or patterns.
- Techniques:
  - Clustering: Groups data into clusters or groups based on similarities (e.g., K-means, DBSCAN).
  - Dimensionality Reduction: Simplifies data by reducing the number of features while preserving essential information (e.g., PCA, t-SNE).

Reinforcement Learning

- Definition: Reinforcement learning trains an agent to make decisions by interacting with an

environment, receiving rewards or punishments based on its actions.
- Techniques:
  - Q-learning: Uses a Q-table to estimate the value of each action in each state.
  - Deep Q Networks (DQN): Combines neural networks with Q-learning to handle complex and continuous environments.

2.4 Neural Networks and Deep Learning

Neural networks and deep learning are at the heart of recent advances in AI, enabling state-of-the-art performance in areas such as computer vision and natural language processing.

Artificial Neural Networks (ANN)

- Structure: Composed of layers of interconnected neurons, where each neuron applies an activation function to a linear combination of its inputs.
- Activation Functions: Sigmoid, ReLU (Rectified Linear Unit), tanh, etc.
- Training: Uses backpropagation to adjust the weights of connections by minimizing a loss function.

Convolutional Neural Networks (CNN)

- Usage: Primarily used for image recognition and computer vision.
-

Layers: Composed of convolutional layers, pooling layers, and fully connected layers.
- Advantages: Capable of capturing spatial features of images.

Recurrent Neural Networks (RNN)

- Usage: Designed to process sequences of data, such as time series and natural language.
- LSTM and GRU: Variants of RNNs that solve the vanishing gradient problem, allowing the learning of long-term dependencies.

2.5 Theories of Learning

Theories of learning provide mathematical and conceptual foundations for AI.

Statistical Learning Theory

- VC Dimension: Measures a model's capacity to correctly classify a set of points.
- Uniform Convergence Theorem: Guarantees that the performance on the training set will be close to the performance on the test set for simple models.

Bayesian Learning

- Principle: Uses Bayesian probability to update beliefs about model parameters based on observed data.

- Algorithms: Naive Bayes, Bayesian graphical models.

2.6 Conclusion

This chapter covered the fundamental theoretical concepts of AI, from algorithms and data structures to machine learning techniques and deep learning. A thorough understanding of these basics is essential for exploring and applying AI effectively. The following chapters will focus on practical applications of these techniques and the impact of AI in various domains.

3. Machine Learning Techniques

3.1 Introduction

Machine learning (ML) is a critical subset of artificial intelligence, focusing on developing algorithms that allow computers to learn from and make decisions based on data. This chapter delves into various machine learning techniques, including supervised learning, unsupervised learning, reinforcement learning, and deep learning.

3.2 Supervised Learning

Supervised learning involves training a model on a labeled dataset, where the outcome or label is known. The goal is to learn a mapping from inputs to outputs that can be used to predict labels for new data.

Linear Regression
- Description: Models the relationship between a dependent variable and one or more independent variables using a linear equation.
- Applications: Predicting continuous values, such as housing prices, sales forecasts.

Logistic Regression

- Description: Used for binary classification problems. Models the probability that a given input belongs to a certain class.
- Applications: Spam detection, disease diagnosis.

Decision Trees

- Description: Uses a tree-like structure to model decisions based on feature values.
- Advantages: Easy to interpret, handles both numerical and categorical data.
- Disadvantages: Prone to overfitting if not pruned properly.

Random Forests

- Description: An ensemble method that combines multiple decision trees to improve accuracy and reduce overfitting.
- Applications: Classification and regression tasks in finance, healthcare, and more.

Support Vector Machines (SVM)

- Description: Finds the hyperplane that best separates the classes in the feature space.
- Applications: Image recognition, text categorization.

3.3 Unsupervised Learning

Unsupervised learning involves training models on data without labeled responses, allowing the algorithm to discover patterns and structures within the data.

Clustering

- K-means Clustering: Partitions data into K clusters, each represented by the mean of its points.
- Hierarchical Clustering: Builds a hierarchy of clusters either agglomeratively or divisively.
- Applications: Customer segmentation, image compression.

Dimensionality Reduction

- Principal Component Analysis (PCA): Reduces the number of features by projecting data onto the directions of maximum variance.
- t-Distributed Stochastic Neighbor Embedding (t-SNE): Visualizes high-dimensional data by reducing it to two or three dimensions.
- Applications: Data visualization, noise reduction.

3.4 Reinforcement Learning

Reinforcement learning (RL) involves training an agent to make decisions by interacting with an environment, receiving rewards or punishments based on its actions.

Q-learning

- Description: An off-policy RL algorithm that learns the value of actions in states to maximize cumulative rewards.
- Applications: Game playing, robotic control.

Deep Q Networks (DQN)

- Description: Combines Q-learning with deep neural networks to handle high-dimensional state spaces.
- Applications: Atari game playing, autonomous driving.

3.5 Deep Learning

Deep learning is a subset of machine learning that uses neural networks with many layers to model complex patterns in data.

Convolutional Neural Networks (CNN)

- Description: Designed for processing grid-like data such as images. Uses convolutional layers to capture spatial hierarchies.
- Applications: Image and video recognition, medical image analysis.

Recurrent Neural Networks (RNN)

- Description: Designed for sequence data. Uses recurrent connections to capture temporal dependencies.
- LSTM and GRU: Variants that address the vanishing gradient problem.
- Applications: Language modeling, speech recognition.

Generative Adversarial Networks (GAN)

- Description: Consists of a generator and a discriminator in a game-theoretic setting. The generator creates data, and the discriminator evaluates its authenticity.
- Applications: Image generation, data augmentation.

3.6 Transfer Learning

Transfer learning involves transferring knowledge from one domain or task to another. It is especially useful when labeled data is scarce in the target domain.

Pre-trained Models

- Description: Using models trained on large datasets (e.g., ImageNet) as a starting point for related tasks.

- Applications: Fine-tuning for specific applications such as object detection and language translation.

3.7 Model Evaluation and Selection

Evaluating and selecting the right model is crucial for successful machine learning applications.

Evaluation Metrics

- Accuracy: Percentage of correctly predicted instances.
- Precision, Recall, F1-score: Metrics for evaluating classification performance, especially in imbalanced datasets.
- ROC-AUC: Measures the ability of a model to distinguish between classes.

Cross-Validation

- Description: Technique for assessing the generalizability of a model by partitioning data into training and validation sets.
- K-fold Cross-Validation: Divides data into K subsets and trains the model K times, each time using a different subset as the validation set.

3.8 Conclusion

This chapter covered a range of machine learning techniques, from supervised and unsupervised learning to reinforcement learning and deep learning. Each technique has its own strengths and applications, making it essential to understand them thoroughly to choose the right approach for a given problem. The next chapter will explore practical applications of these techniques across various domains.

4. Applications of AI

4.1 Introduction

Artificial Intelligence has a broad range of applications across different industries and fields. This chapter explores how AI is transforming various sectors, including healthcare, finance, transportation, and more.

4.2 Healthcare

AI is revolutionizing healthcare by enhancing diagnostic accuracy, personalizing treatment plans, and improving patient care.

Medical Imaging

- Applications: AI algorithms analyze medical images (e.g., X-rays, MRIs) to detect abnormalities such as tumors, fractures, and infections.
- Example: Google's DeepMind developed an AI system that can diagnose eye diseases with high accuracy.

Personalized Medicine

- Applications: AI analyzes patient data to tailor treatments to individual needs, predicting which therapies will be most effective.
- Example: IBM Watson for Oncology provides evidence-based treatment recommendations.

Drug Discovery

- Applications: AI accelerates the drug discovery process by predicting the efficacy of new compounds and identifying potential drug targets.
- Example: BenevolentAI uses AI to discover new drugs and repurpose existing ones.

4.3 Finance

AI is transforming the finance industry by improving risk management, automating trading, and enhancing customer service.

Algorithmic Trading

- Applications: AI algorithms analyze market data in real-time to execute trades at optimal prices, often faster and more accurately than human traders.
- Example: Quantitative hedge funds use AI to develop trading strategies based on historical data.

Fraud Detection

- Applications: AI systems detect fraudulent transactions by identifying patterns and anomalies in large datasets.
- Example: PayPal uses AI to monitor transactions and flag suspicious activities.

Customer Service

- Applications: AI-powered chatbots and virtual assistants provide customer support, answering queries and resolving issues efficiently.
- Example: Bank of America's Erica is an AI-driven virtual assistant that helps customers manage their finances.

4.4 Transportation

AI is enhancing transportation systems by improving safety, optimizing routes, and enabling autonomous vehicles.

Autonomous Vehicles

- Applications: AI enables self-driving cars to navigate, make decisions, and interact with their environment.
- Example: Tesla's Autopilot system uses AI to assist with driving tasks such as lane-keeping and adaptive cruise control.

Traffic Management

- Applications: AI optimizes traffic flow and reduces congestion by analyzing real-time data from sensors and cameras.
- Example: Cities like Los Angeles use AI to adjust traffic light timings based on traffic conditions.

Logistics and Supply Chain

- Applications: AI optimizes supply chain operations by predicting demand, managing inventory, and planning routes.
- Example: Amazon uses AI to forecast product demand and streamline its logistics network.

4.5 Retail

AI is transforming the retail industry by enhancing customer experiences, optimizing inventory management, and personalizing marketing.

Personalized Recommendations

- Applications: AI analyzes customer data to provide personalized product recommendations, improving customer satisfaction and increasing sales.
- Example: Amazon's recommendation engine suggests products based on browsing and purchase history.

Inventory Management

- Applications: AI predicts demand for products and optimizes inventory levels to reduce stockouts and overstocking.
- Example: Walmart uses AI to forecast demand and manage its inventory more efficiently.

Customer Service

- Applications: AI-powered chatbots and virtual assistants handle customer inquiries, providing quick and accurate responses.
- Example: H&M's chatbot assists customers with product searches and order tracking.

4.6 Manufacturing

AI is driving innovation in manufacturing by improving quality control, predictive maintenance, and supply chain optimization.

Quality Control

- Applications: AI systems inspect products for defects and ensure they meet quality standards.
- Example: Siemens uses AI for visual inspection of products, detecting defects with high accuracy.

Predictive Maintenance

- Applications: AI predicts equipment failures and schedules maintenance to prevent downtime and extend machinery lifespan.
- Example: GE uses AI to monitor and predict maintenance needs for its industrial equipment.

Supply Chain Optimization

- Applications: AI optimizes supply chain processes by forecasting demand, managing inventory, and planning logistics.
- Example: Procter & Gamble uses AI to optimize its supply chain and reduce operational costs.

4.7 Education

AI is enhancing education by personalizing learning experiences, automating administrative tasks, and providing insights into student performance.

Personalized Learning

- Applications: AI adapts educational content to individual student needs, providing personalized learning paths and resources.
- Example: Duolingo uses AI to tailor language lessons to each learner's proficiency level.

Administrative Tasks

- Applications: AI automates administrative tasks such as grading, scheduling, and attendance tracking, allowing educators to focus on teaching.
- Example: Turnitin uses AI to grade essays and provide feedback on student writing.

Student Performance Analysis

- Applications: AI analyzes student data to identify learning patterns, predict performance, and provide actionable insights.
- Example: Knewton uses AI to analyze student performance and recommend personalized study materials.

4.8 Entertainment

AI is transforming the entertainment industry by creating new forms of content, personalizing recommendations, and enhancing user experiences.

Content Creation

- Applications: AI generates music, art, and even scripts, opening up new possibilities for creative expression.
- Example: OpenAI's GPT-3 can generate human-like text, including stories and dialogues.

Personalized Recommendations

- Applications: AI recommends movies, music, and other content based on user preferences and behavior.
- Example: Netflix uses AI to recommend shows and movies tailored to individual viewing habits.

Enhanced User Experiences

- Applications: AI creates immersive and interactive experiences in games and virtual environments.
- Example: AI-powered NPCs (non-player characters) in video games adapt their behavior based on player actions.

4.9 Conclusion

AI is having a transformative impact across a wide range of industries, improving efficiency, enhancing customer experiences, and creating new opportunities. Understanding these applications helps us appreciate the potential of AI and its role in shaping the future. The next chapter will discuss the real-world implementation of AI, including challenges and considerations.

5. AI in the Real World

5.1 Introduction

Implementing AI in real-world scenarios involves navigating a range of practical challenges and considerations. This chapter explores the practical aspects of deploying AI, including data management, model development, deployment, and monitoring.

5.2 Data Management

Data is the foundation of AI. Effective data management is crucial for developing accurate and reliable AI models.

Data Collection
- Sources: Data can be collected from various sources, including sensors, user interactions, and publicly available datasets.
- Considerations: Ensuring data quality, relevance, and representativeness is essential for building effective models.

Data Preprocessing
- Cleaning: Removing noise, handling missing values, and correcting errors.

- Transformation: Normalizing, scaling, and encoding features to prepare data for modeling.
- Augmentation: Generating additional data through techniques like oversampling and synthetic data creation.

Data Storage

- Databases: Relational databases (e.g., MySQL) and NoSQL databases (e.g., MongoDB) for structured and unstructured data.
- Data Lakes: Centralized repositories that store raw data in its native format, supporting large-scale data analytics.

5.3 Model Development

Developing AI models involves selecting the right algorithms, tuning hyperparameters, and evaluating performance.

Algorithm Selection

- Criteria: Choosing algorithms based on the problem type (e.g., classification, regression), data size, and computational resources.
- Popular Algorithms: Decision trees, support vector machines, neural networks, etc.

Hyperparameter Tuning

- Definition: Adjusting algorithm parameters to optimize model performance.
- Techniques: Grid search, random search, and Bayesian optimization.

Model Training

- Process: Splitting data into training and validation sets, training the model on the training set, and tuning based on validation performance.
- Challenges: Avoiding overfitting and underfitting, ensuring sufficient computational resources.

5.4 Deployment

Deploying AI models into production requires careful planning to ensure scalability, reliability, and security.

Model Serving

- Techniques: Using APIs, microservices, and serverless architectures to serve models.
- Tools: TensorFlow Serving, AWS SageMaker, and Kubernetes.

Scalability

- Considerations: Ensuring the system can handle increasing data volumes and user requests.

- Approaches: Load balancing, distributed computing, and cloud-based solutions.

Security
- Concerns: Protecting sensitive data, preventing model theft, and ensuring robustness against adversarial attacks.
- Measures: Encryption, access controls, and regular security audits.

5.5 Monitoring and Maintenance

Continuous monitoring and maintenance are essential to ensure AI models remain accurate and reliable over time.

Performance Monitoring
- Metrics: Tracking model performance using metrics such as accuracy, precision, recall, and F1-score.
- Tools: Monitoring platforms like Prometheus, Grafana, and ELK stack.

Model Retraining
- Need: Updating models to adapt to new data and changing environments.
- Process: Periodic retraining using recent data, automating the retraining pipeline.

Error Analysis

- Importance: Identifying and analyzing errors to improve model performance.
- Techniques: Confusion matrix, error distribution analysis, and root cause analysis.

5.6 Ethical and Legal Considerations

Implementing AI in the real world involves addressing ethical and legal challenges to ensure fairness, transparency, and accountability.

Bias and Fairness

- Issue: AI models can inherit biases from training data, leading to unfair outcomes.
- Approaches: Auditing data for bias, implementing fairness-aware algorithms, and promoting diversity in AI development.

Transparency and Explainability

- Importance: Ensuring AI decisions are understandable and explainable to users and stakeholders.
- Techniques: Using interpretable models, visualizing decision processes, and providing explanations.

Privacy and Security

- Concerns: Protecting user data and ensuring compliance with privacy regulations.
- Measures: Implementing data anonymization, secure data storage, and adhering to laws like GDPR and CCPA.

5.7 Conclusion

Implementing AI in the real world requires careful consideration of data management, model development, deployment, and ethical issues. By addressing these challenges, organizations can effectively leverage AI to drive innovation and achieve their goals. The next chapter will delve into the ethical and societal implications of AI.

6. Ethics and Challenges of AI

6.1 Introduction

As AI continues to advance, it brings with it significant ethical and societal challenges. This chapter explores the ethical implications of AI, including issues of bias, privacy, transparency, and the potential impact on employment and society at large.

6.2 Bias and Fairness

Bias in AI systems can lead to unfair and discriminatory outcomes, affecting individuals and groups disproportionately.

Sources of Bias

- Data Bias: Historical and societal biases present in training data.
- Algorithmic Bias: Bias introduced by the algorithms themselves, often due to design choices or assumptions.

Mitigating Bias

- Data Auditing: Regularly auditing training data for bias and ensuring diverse and representative datasets.
- Fair Algorithms: Developing and implementing fairness-aware algorithms that reduce or eliminate bias.
- Transparency: Providing clear explanations of how AI systems make decisions to identify and address biases.

6.3 Privacy and Security

AI systems often rely on vast amounts of personal data, raising significant privacy and security concerns.

Data Privacy

- Concerns: Unauthorized access to personal data, data breaches, and misuse of sensitive information.
- Measures: Implementing robust data protection practices, encryption, and anonymization techniques.

Security Risks

- Threats: Hacking, adversarial attacks, and malicious use of AI technologies.
- Approaches: Enhancing cybersecurity measures, developing robust AI models resistant to attacks, and conducting regular security audits.

6.4 Transparency and Explainability

Ensuring AI systems are transparent and their decisions explainable is crucial for building trust and accountability.

Importance

- Trust: Users are more likely to trust AI systems if they understand how decisions are made.
- Accountability: Clear explanations allow for accountability in the event of errors or adverse outcomes.

Techniques

- Interpretable Models: Using simpler, more interpretable models where possible.
- Explanation Tools: Developing tools and methods to provide explanations for complex models (e.g., LIME, SHAP).

6.5 Impact on Employment

AI has the potential to significantly impact employment, both by creating new opportunities and displacing existing jobs.

Job Displacement

- Concerns: Automation of tasks leading to job losses, particularly in low-skill roles.

- Sectors Affected: Manufacturing, retail, transportation, and customer service.

Job Creation

- Opportunities: New jobs in AI development, data science, and related fields.
- Reskilling: Importance of reskilling and upskilling workers to adapt to the changing job landscape.

6.6 Societal Impact

The widespread adoption of AI can have profound societal implications, both positive and negative.

Positive Impacts

- Healthcare: Improved diagnostics, personalized treatments, and better patient outcomes.
- Environment: AI-driven solutions for climate change, resource management, and sustainability.
- Education: Personalized learning, better student engagement, and improved educational outcomes.

Negative Impacts

- Inequality: Potential to exacerbate existing inequalities if benefits are not widely distributed.
- Surveillance: Increased surveillance and loss of privacy, particularly in authoritarian regimes.
- Autonomy: Ethical concerns about the autonomy of AI systems and their decision-making processes.

6.7 Ethical Frameworks and Guidelines

Developing ethical frameworks and guidelines is essential for ensuring the responsible development and deployment of AI.

Principles

- Fairness: Ensuring AI systems are fair and do not discriminate.
- Accountability: Establishing clear accountability for AI decisions and outcomes.
- Transparency: Promoting transparency in AI development and deployment.
- Privacy: Protecting individual privacy and data security.

Organizations and Initiatives

- AI Ethics Guidelines: Various organizations have developed guidelines for ethical AI (e.g., IEEE, European Commission).
- Collaborations: Multistakeholder collaborations to address ethical challenges and promote responsible AI (e.g., Partnership on AI).

6.8 Conclusion

Addressing the ethical and societal challenges of AI is crucial for its responsible development and deployment. By considering issues of bias, privacy, transparency, and the broader impact on society, we can ensure that AI technologies benefit everyone. The final chapter will discuss the future of AI and its potential trajectory.

7. The Future of AI

7.1 Introduction

The future of AI is full of promise and potential, with advancements poised to transform various aspects of our lives. This chapter explores emerging trends, potential breakthroughs, and the long-term impact of AI on society.

7.2 Emerging Trends

Several emerging trends are shaping the future of AI, pushing the boundaries of what is possible.

AI and Internet of Things (IoT)
- Integration: Combining AI with IoT to create intelligent systems that can process and analyze data from connected devices in real-time.
- Applications: Smart homes, industrial automation, and predictive maintenance.

Edge AI
- Concept: Moving AI processing to the edge of the network, closer to where data is generated.

- Advantages: Reduced latency, improved privacy, and decreased reliance on centralized cloud infrastructure.
- Applications: Autonomous vehicles, smart cameras, and real-time analytics.

AI in Healthcare

- Advancements: Continued improvement in AI-driven diagnostics, personalized medicine, and drug discovery.
- Impact: Enhanced patient care, faster treatment development, and more efficient healthcare systems.

Natural Language Processing (NLP)

- Progress: Advances in NLP, enabling more accurate language understanding and generation.
- Applications: Improved virtual assistants, automated content creation, and enhanced translation services.

7.3 Potential Breakthroughs

Several potential breakthroughs could significantly advance the field of AI, leading to new capabilities and applications.

General AI

- Goal: Developing AI systems with general intelligence, capable of performing a wide range of tasks across different domains.
- Challenges: Addressing issues of adaptability, reasoning, and understanding.

Quantum Computing and AI

- Synergy: Leveraging quantum computing to enhance AI algorithms, enabling faster processing and solving complex problems.
- Potential: Improved optimization, better drug discovery, and advanced materials science.

Brain-Computer Interfaces (BCI)

- Concept: Directly connecting AI systems to the human brain, enabling seamless interaction and control.
- Applications: Assistive technologies for individuals with disabilities, enhanced cognitive abilities, and new forms of human-computer interaction.

7.4 Long-Term Impact

The long-term impact of AI will shape society in profound ways, influencing various aspects of our lives and the global economy.

Economic Transformation

- Productivity: Increased productivity and efficiency across industries, driving economic growth.
- Job Market: Shift in job market dynamics, with new roles emerging and others becoming obsolete.

Societal Changes

- Quality of Life: Improvements in healthcare, education, and daily living through AI-driven innovations.
- Ethical Considerations: Ongoing need to address ethical challenges and ensure the equitable distribution of AI benefits.

Global Collaboration

- Collaboration: Increased collaboration between countries, organizations, and researchers to address global challenges and promote responsible AI.
- Regulation: Development of international standards and regulations to govern the use of AI.

- **7.5 Conclusion**

The future of AI holds immense potential, with emerging trends, potential breakthroughs, and long-term impacts shaping our world. By understanding these developments and addressing the associated challenges, we can harness the power of AI to create a better future for all.

Glossary

- Algorithm: A step-by-step procedure or formula for solving a problem.
- Artificial Neural Network (ANN): A computational model inspired by the way biological neural networks in the human brain process information.
- Bias: Systematic error introduced into data or algorithms that can lead to unfair or discriminatory outcomes.
- Convolutional Neural Network (CNN): A type of neural network designed for processing structured grid data, such as images.
- Data Preprocessing: The process of cleaning, transforming, and preparing raw data for analysis.
- Deep Learning: A subset of machine learning that uses neural networks with many layers to model complex patterns in data.
- Hyperparameter: A parameter whose value is set before the learning process begins and used to control the learning process.
- Internet of Things (IoT): A network of interconnected devices that communicate and exchange data.
- Machine Learning (ML): A subset of AI that involves the development of algorithms that allow computers to learn from and make predictions based on data.

- Natural Language Processing (NLP): A field of AI that focuses on the interaction between computers and human language.

- Overfitting: A modeling error that occurs when a model is too closely fit to a limited set of data points, resulting in poor generalization to new data.

- Reinforcement Learning (RL): A type of machine learning where an agent learns to make decisions by interacting with an environment and receiving rewards or punishments.

- Supervised Learning: A type of machine learning where the model is trained on labeled data, learning to predict the output from the input data.

- Unsupervised Learning: A type of machine learning where the model is trained on unlabeled data and must find patterns and structures in the input data.

References

- Goodfellow, I., Bengio, Y., & Courville, A. (2016). Deep Learning. MIT Press.
- Bishop, C. M. (2006). Pattern Recognition and Machine Learning. Springer.
- Russell, S. J., & Norvig, P. (2016). Artificial Intelligence: A Modern Approach. Pearson.
- Silver, D., Huang, A., Maddison, C. J., et al. (2016). Mastering the game of Go with deep neural networks and tree search. Nature, 529(7587), 484-489.
- LeCun, Y., Bengio, Y., & Hinton, G. (2015). Deep learning. Nature, 521(7553), 436-444.
- Chollet, F. (2017). Deep Learning with Python. Manning Publications.

www.ingramcontent.com/pod-product-compliance
Lightning Source LLC
Chambersburg PA
CBHW071959210526
45479CB00003B/1003